THE Couples Therapy *Flip Chart*

A PSYCHOEDUCATIONAL TOOL TO HELP COUPLES IDENTIFY PATTERNS OF DISCONNECTION, MANAGE RELATIONSHIP CONFLICT, AND CREATE A THRIVING PARTNERSHIP

ELIZABETH EARNSHAW, LMFT, CGT

The Couples Therapy Flip Chart

Published by
PESI Publishing, Inc.
3839 White Ave
Eau Claire, WI 54703

Cover and interior design by Emily Dyer
Editing by Chelsea Thompson

ISBN 9781683737131 (print)
ISBN 9781683737155 (ePDF)
ISBN 9781683737148 (KPF)

Printed in the United States of America.

PESI Publishing
pesipublishing.com

About the Author

Elizabeth Earnshaw, LMFT, CGT, is a marriage and family therapist, clinical fellow of the American Association of Marriage and Family Therapy (AAMFT), certified Gottman Method couples therapist, certified clinical trauma professional, and AAMFT-approved supervisor. She is the author of the bestselling relationship book *I Want This to Work* and the owner of a national therapy practice that provides systemic therapy to individuals, couples, and families. Elizabeth has worked with hundreds of couples since becoming a couples therapist. She lives in West Chester, Pennsylvania, with her husband, children, and dog.

Introduction

The Couples Therapy Flip Chart is designed to support therapists in illustrating and explaining key concepts in couples therapy. Divided into the following four sections, this flip chart will support your work with couples in identifying patterns of disconnection, building new communication and conflict resolution skills, and creating a more satisfying relationship:

1. **Understanding Each Other:** This section highlights key areas that often cause conflict between couples due to misunderstandings about how each individual thinks, processes information, or navigates conflict. The goal is not to make each individual the same, but rather to help them identify, appreciate, and accept their differences.
2. **Managing Conflict:** Most couples enter therapy because they are unhappy with conflict within their relationship. This section helps couples better understand what causes conflict to escalate and, rather than eradicate conflict altogether, learn how to de-escalate and manage it.
3. **Creating a Secure Relationship:** Many issues in relationships arise because couples do not know how to manage their partnership in relation to the outside world and the risks that accompany it. Because of this, they create insecurity within their relationship, which can lead to resentment and betrayal. This section provides psychoeducation on how to create a secure relationship.
4. **Daily Life:** Relationships require daily effort and care. This section highlights what couples should be mindful of in daily life to create a thriving relationship.

On each page, you will find a black-and-white therapist-facing side, which includes key concepts and guidance for explaining each concept in session, as well as a colorful laminated couples-facing side, which includes additional images, checklists, or explanations for your clients. You can use dry-erase markers on the couples-facing pages to customize the chart to each couple and reuse the pages across multiple sessions.

The work we do with couples sets the foundation for our families, communities, and society to thrive. Each insight we help to instill, each harmful pattern we help to shift, is a stepping stone toward a better future for us all. I hope that these resources serve you well in your practice—I wish you all the best in this vital work.

Elizabeth Earnshaw, LMFT, CGT

Table of Contents

Relationship Phases

Relationships evolve through four phases:

- **Honeymoon phase:** Idealization, creates a base for fond memories, minimization of "issues"
- **Realization phase:** Private distress begins to grow as partners analyze and worry about what the differences between them mean for themselves and the relationship
- **Tension phase:** Minimization of the positive, power struggles emerge, partners resist differences
- **Acceptance phase:** Acceptance grows, moving from control to tolerance, negotiation, and appreciation of differences

Session Guidance

- ***Assessment:***
  - Have the couple reflect on the honeymoon stage to encourage positive memories/maintenance of positive thoughts and to better understand how they see their past (negative or positive).
  - Work with the couple to identify which phase they are stuck in.
- ***Intervention:***
  - Encourage the couple to understand each other's differences. Share with the couple that there will always be differences but that an important part of a healthy relationship is accepting, respecting, and negotiating them.
  - Normalize differences; emphasize acceptance over sameness.

Relationship Phases

Which Phase Are You In?

Circle the phase that best describes your relationship right now:

Honeymoon	Realization
Idolize	Notice
Fantasize	Analyze
Excuse	Worry

Tension	Acceptance
Criticize	Tolerate
Magnify	Negotiate
Control	Appreciate

Acceptance = I am me and you are you and we both are good enough.

What's your favorite honeymoon phase memory? ________________________________

____

____

Describe why you think you're stuck in the phase you circled: ________________________

____

____

The Tortoise and the Hare

This common couple combination highlights differences between partners that can cause misunderstandings.

Tortoises	Hares
• Are unlikely to share information • Need time to ponder their responses to questions • Withdraw when emotions and conflict are present	• Spontaneously share information • Are fast-paced in their questions and responses • Pursue when their partner withdraws
Tortoises need to: • "Stick out their neck" by working to share information • Be verbal about their needs for space instead of just withdrawing	**Hares need to:** • Slow down and breathe • Give their partner a warning when they want to discuss something ("I would like to talk about [*issue*] … can we talk tonight?")

Session Guidance

- ***Assessment & Psychoeducation:*** Identify and explain the tortoise/hare dynamic.
- ***Intervention:***
  - Help each partner develop empathy for the other by pointing out the emotional experience—the tortoise is feeling overwhelmed; the hare is feeling anxious.
  - Coach each person toward meeting in the middle. Help the tortoise ask for space or share thoughts and feelings; help the hare slow down and offer space.

The Tortoise and the Hare

Communication Differences

Partner A, put a star next to the traits that resonate with you. Partner B, put a check mark next to the traits that resonate with you.

Tortoises Tend To:	Hares Tend To:
❑ Share slowly	❑ Share quickly
❑ Need time to ponder	❑ Be spontaneous communicators
❑ Withdraw when stressed	❑ Think on their feet
❑ Need space	❑ Need reassurance
❑ Be more succinct	❑ Be more verbose

How does it affect you when these qualities show up in your relationship?

The goal:
Meet in the middle.
Tortoises need to stick their head out of their shell.
Hares need to slow down.

Describe one thing each of you can do to begin to meet in the middle:

Partner A:	Partner B:

The Solution Coach versus the Emotion Coach

Many couples include a solution coach and an emotion coach during conflict. This difference can cause misunderstandings and lead to criticism and conflict. To avoid conflict, couples can identify the difference and learn how to meet in the middle.

The Solution Coach	The Emotion Coach
• Prioritizes solutions over feelings • Dismissive of emotions • Motivated toward progress	• Values expressing feelings • Frustrated by immediate solutions • Knows how to create emotional connection

Session Guidance

- ***Assessment & Psychoeducation:*** Identify and explain the solution coach/emotion coach dynamic.
- ***Intervention:***
    - Encourage each individual to learn from the other person. The emotion coach can learn to be more forward-thinking and the solution coach can learn to be more in touch with emotions.
    - When you notice that a solution coach/emotion coach interaction is causing conflict, point it out and guide the couple to work with each other's styles.

The Solution Coach versus the Emotion Coach

How Partners Respond During Difficult Moments

Partner A, put a star next to each quality that you think accurately describes you. Partner B, put a check mark next to each quality that you think accurately describes you.

The Solution Coach	The Emotion Coach
❑ Believes sharing feelings is mostly unhelpful when it comes to navigating stress	❑ Believes that sharing feelings is incredibly helpful when navigating stress
❑ Finds solutions to be soothing when navigating difficulty	❑ Finds solutions to be unhelpful or frustrating when initially navigating difficulty
❑ Wants to give and receive solutions	❑ Wants to give and receive empathy
❑ Tends to be dismissive in response to emotions	❑ Tends to be dismissive in response to solutions
❑ Is able to see the "way out" of the issue	❑ Is able to see the impact of the issue
❑ Talented at creating forward movement	❑ Talented at creating connection

The goal:
Instead of solution coach versus emotion coach, become a solution coach *and* an emotion coach.

Philosophies

Dr. John Gottman's research found that 69 percent of conflicts are unsolvable.* When you work with couples, you find that these unsolvable issues are usually the result of differing life philosophies.

Example: Spender versus Saver

The spender believes life is short and you should enjoy your money while you're here; the saver believes life is uncertain and it's important to be prepared for the future.

Couples can respect each other's philosophy through negotiation.

Example: Create separate accounts—one for spending and one for saving.

Session Guidance

- ***Assessment:*** Point out when the couple has a philosophical difference.
- ***Psychoeducation:*** Normalize differences and show them the list of possible differences.
- ***Coaching:*** Encourage each person to tolerate differing points of view. Have the couple talk with each other about their personal POV while guiding them toward understanding the other's. You can help the couple start the conversation by asking them to talk about what they believe people "should" do regarding the issue.
- ***Problem-Solving:*** Help the couple learn to negotiate by coming up with creative solutions that take each person's needs into account. (The final page of this chart presents a framework for negotiation.)

* Gottman, J. M., & Silver, N. (2015). *The seven principles for making marriage work: A practical guide from the country's foremost relationship expert* (Rev. ed.). Harmony Books.

Philosophies

Common Philosophical Differences

Put a check mark next to any differences in your relationship:

- ❑ Political views
- ❑ Parenting styles
- ❑ Financial beliefs
- ❑ Religious beliefs
- ❑ The purpose of life
- ❑ Work/life balance
- ❑ Conflict styles
- ❑ Beliefs about tidiness and cleanliness
- ❑ Beliefs about socializing
- ❑ Beliefs about the use of leisure time
- ❑ Beliefs about moral rights and wrongs
- ❑ Beliefs about in-laws and family dynamics
- ❑ Beliefs about sex and intimacy
- ❑ ____________________
- ❑ ____________________

Rank the top three differences that cause the most conflict in your relationship:

1. ____________________
2. ____________________
3. ____________________

The Dual Control Model*

The mind has two parts for intimacy and desire:

- **Accelerator:** This part propels emotional and sexual closeness, increasing motivation for intimacy.
- **Brake:** This part slows desire, causing caution in getting too close, even if you care about your partner.

These parts work together, responding to feelings, thoughts, and surroundings. Depending on the person and situation, sometimes the accelerator is stronger; other times the brake is more prominent. Being aware of what's driving or stopping your feelings helps you connect with your partner and build a more satisfying relationship.

For couples to have a healthy sexual relationship, it is important to understand and respect each other's differences regarding desire.

Session Guidance

- ***Psychoeducation:*** Explain the dual control model to couples with libido concerns.
- ***Interventions:***
    - ***Intimacy Map:*** Partners create diagrams labeling accelerators (closeness triggers) and brakes (intimacy hurdles).
    - ***Desire Diary:*** Partners track accelerators and brakes, situations, emotions, and reactions.
    - ***Sexual Menu:*** Partners make a list of comfortable sexual activities, grouped by accelerators and brakes.

*Adapted from:

Bancroft, J., Graham, C. A., Janssen, E., & Sanders, S. A. (2009). The dual control model: current status and future directions. *Journal of Sex Research, 46*(2–3), 121–142.

Nagoski, E. (2021). *Come as you are: Revised and updated: The surprising new science that will transform your sex life.* Simon & Schuster.

Dual Control Model

Accelerators	Brakes
• ***Physical attraction:*** Smells, clothing, body parts • ***Positive thoughts:*** Positive memories of past sexual experiences, positive body image, positive thoughts about the relationship • ***Emotional connection:*** Feeling understood, sharing feelings, feeling supported • ***Novelty:*** Trying something new together • ***Environment:*** Cleanliness, mood lighting, a specific place (the bedroom, a hotel, etc.)	• ***Lack of attraction:*** Bad odors, unattractive images • ***Stress:*** Work, health, finances, parenting, relationship, mental load • ***Negative thoughts:*** Feeling insecure about yourself or the relationship, body image issues, lack of confidence, negative thoughts about your partner, negative memories of past sexual experiences • ***Distractions:*** Your phone, work, other responsibilities • ***Environment:*** Messiness, a specific place (being at home, etc.)

Exploring Our Accelerators and Brakes

Trauma and Relationships

Trauma is a response to a distressing event or series of events that were experienced as especially physically or emotionally harmful. When one or more members of a relationship have experienced trauma, the trauma might manifest within the relationship when triggered.

When couples understand each other's trauma and are aware of each other's triggers, they can respond to each other with sensitivity and care. By doing this, they are providing each other a safe environment in which to heal from trauma and reducing the likelihood that conflicts escalate due to trauma responses.

Session Guidance

- ***Psychoeducation:*** If you notice that one or more members of the relationship are having a trauma response, provide psychoeducation to both members of the couple about trauma and triggers.
- ***Intervention:*** Guide the couple to discuss the triggers related to their traumatic experience. Have them describe the trigger, what usually activates it, and what helps when they are triggered.

Trauma and Relationships

Trigger: A situation, word, or feeling that reminds one of a traumatic experience (or experiences). When triggered, a person might manifest:

Hyperarousal	Hypoarousal
• Agitation	• Muted response
• Criticism	• Stonewalling
• Defensiveness	• Withdrawn
• Reactivity	• Numb
• Pursuit	• Avoidance

Trust: People who have experienced trauma might struggle to trust their partner, even if nothing untrustworthy has happened. It can help to talk about your triggers to build trust.

Here are some things that might trigger a trauma response related to a past experience. Put a check mark by any triggers that relate to you:

- ❑ Raised voice
- ❑ Physical touch/contact
- ❑ Perceived attempts to control
- ❑ Disagreement
- ❑ Harsh words
- ❑ Loud noises
- ❑ Stress
- ❑ Sensory aspects, like smells or lighting
- ❑ Perceived abandonment (e.g., not being able to get in touch on their phone)
- ❑ Substance use (e.g., seeing their partner drink)
- ❑ Financial hardship
- ❑ Physical aggression (even if not directed toward the individual)
- ❑ ________________________________
- ❑ ________________________________

Communication Styles

In conflicts, people typically use one of three communication styles:

- **Passive communication** involves avoiding conflict and suppressing one's feelings. This often leads to resentment.
- **Assertive communication** involves healthy boundaries and honest communication. This allows individuals to express themselves clearly and respectfully, fostering mutual understanding.
- **Aggressive communication** is confrontational and can harm relationships through shouting, insults, or sarcasm.

Many couples in couples therapy use some combination of passive and aggressive communication.

Identifying which form each partner uses can help them to improve their communication.

Session Guidance

- ***Assessment:*** During assessment, pay attention to the communication styles used.
- ***Identification:*** When you notice the couple utilizing passive, aggressive, or assertive communication, pause the conversation and point it out.
- ***Psychoeducation:*** Ask them to use the checklist to better understand their communication styles.
- ***Practice:*** Help the clients to catch themselves when using passive or aggressive communication and practice assertiveness. You can guide them by providing example statements.

Communication Styles

The Goldilocks Spectrum of Communication

Passive — Assertive — Aggressive

Passive Communication

"I will be uncomfortable so you aren't."

- ❑ Avoids conflict
- ❑ Prioritizes others' needs above your own
- ❑ Difficulty expressing thoughts, feelings, and needs
- ❑ Uses phrases like "I'm fine" and "it's okay" even when not true
- ❑ Leads to resentment and frustration

Assertive Communication

"I will handle my own discomfort and expect you to handle yours."

- ❑ Able to face conflict
- ❑ Expresses thoughts, feelings, and needs
- ❑ Able to express yourself and listen to the other person
- ❑ Uses "I" statements and avoids criticism and blame
- ❑ Creates relationship safety and understanding

Aggressive Communication

"I am uncomfortable so I will make you uncomfortable too."

- ❑ Forceful and domineering behavior in conflict
- ❑ Unable to express thoughts, feelings, and needs in an honest and vulnerable manner
- ❑ Struggles to listen to the other side
- ❑ May shout, blame, belittle, or use sarcasm to express thoughts
- ❑ Leads to distant relationships

Conflict Mapping

When couples are in conflict, they are likely utilizing one of three patterns:

- **Pursue/pursue** couples point fingers and feel that winning is more important than resolution.
- **Pursue/withdraw** couples have opposing needs to resolve anxiety—one needs resolution *now* and the other needs space *now*.
- **Withdraw/withdraw** couples were likely stuck in one of the first two patterns previously and now feel exhausted and defeated.

It is important for each partner to recognize which role they most commonly take.

Pursue/Pursue	Pursue/Withdraw	Withdraw/Withdraw
• About winning • Blame game • Reactivity • Look for the "bad guy"	• One talks; one needs space • Both feel anxious and overwhelmed • Pursuer needs the issue to be resolved • Withdrawer needs to know things won't escalate	• Checked out • No one brings up issues • Defeated • Lonely

Session Guidance

- ***Psychoeducation:*** Guide the couple to discuss what role they each tend to take in an argument. Remind them that this is not about blame, but rather about understanding.
- ***Intervention:*** When you notice the couple utilizing pursue or withdraw behaviors, coach them to address their anxiety first and then practice assertive communication.

Conflict Mapping

Noticing What You Do

Pursue/Pursue

- About winning
- Both are reactive
- Blame game (looking for the "bad guy")

Pursue/Withdraw

- Talk versus space
- Both feel anxious and overwhelmed
- Pursuer needs to know the issue will be resolved; withdrawer needs space

---

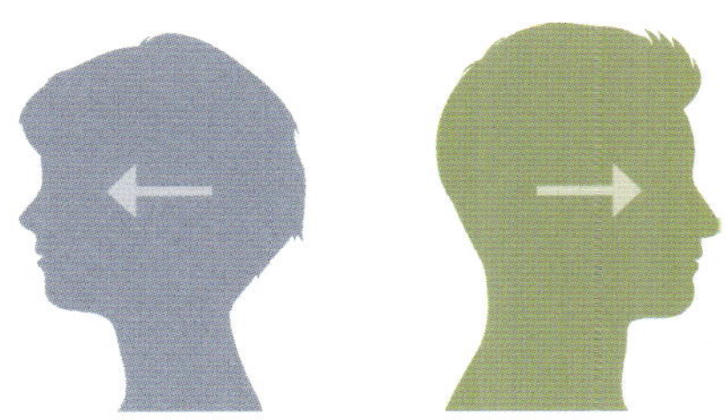

Withdraw/Withdraw

- Checked out
- No one brings up issues
- Defeated and exhausted

Self-Soothing

When people are in conflict, the body responds as if it is under threat, releasing stress hormones that put them into a state of fight, flight, or freeze. This state of emergency in the brain limits capacity for affection, humor, problem-solving, and curiosity. When one member of a couple goes into fight/flight/freeze during conflict, both partners are less able to engage effectively with each other.

Instead of continuing to engage in the conflict, coach couples to disengage from conversations when there are signs of fight, flight, or freeze and to give each other breaks when needed. In addition, couples should learn the important skill of *self-soothing* to navigate this state before attempting to resolve the conflict.

Some simple ways to practice self-soothing:

- **Breath:** Breathing is our body's natural relaxant. A good technique is *box breathing*: Inhale deeply for 4 seconds, hold for 4, exhale for 4, and hold for 4. Repeat.
- **Relaxation:** Tense and relax your muscles from feet to head. This is called *progressive muscle relaxation*. Tighten each muscle group for 5 seconds, then release.
- **Distraction:** Shift focus from distressing thoughts to engaging tasks or mantras. You might take a walk, write or draw in a journal, or get some cleaning done.

Session Guidance

- ***Intervention:*** When you notice that either partner is in a distressed state, ask them to stop and take a break.
- ***Practice:*** Help the couple practice self-soothing in the room. Do not overexplain self-soothing; instead, take them through the experience.
- ***Psychoeducation:*** At the end of the relaxation experience, educate both partners on how important it is to self-soothe.

Self-Soothing

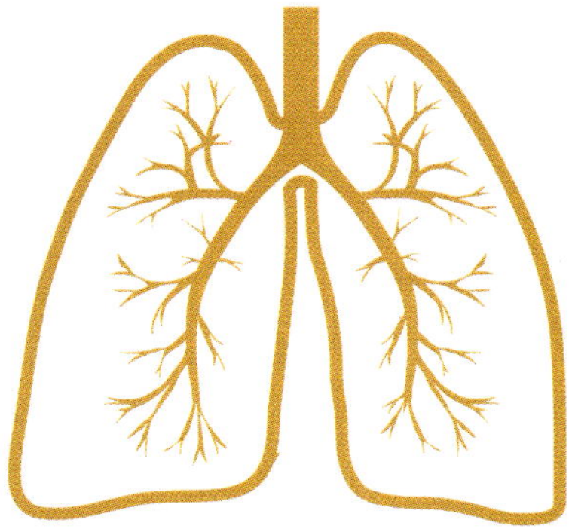

Breath: Practice box breathing (inhale 4, hold 4, exhale 4, hold 4).

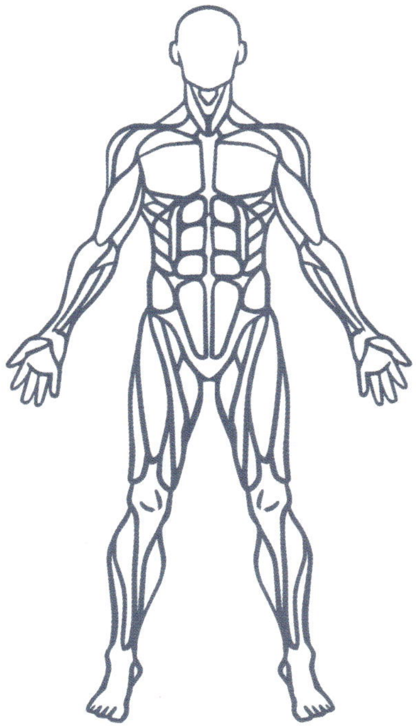

Relaxation: Tense and loosen each muscle group for 5 seconds.

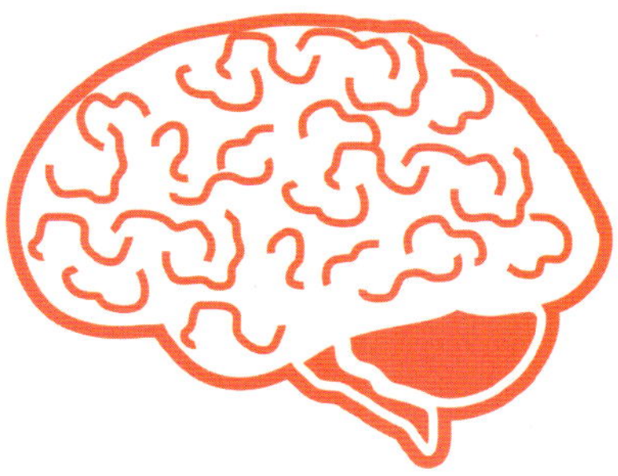

Distraction: Take a walk, write or draw in a journal, get some cleaning done, etc.

Communication Guidelines

Active listening is a foundational skill in relationships. Active listening can be particularly hard during conflict, so it should be practiced during moments of calm to "build the muscle."

Most couples struggle with this skill and could benefit from practicing it in and out of session. When done effectively, active listening promotes better understanding, reduces misunderstandings, and enhances the quality of communication and connection between individuals.

When sharing, it is also important to understand how to be an effective speaker and avoid "losing your listener." You lose your listener when you speak for too long, choose the wrong time, use blame or criticism, or are unclear about what you want or need from the conversation.

Session Guidance

- ***Practice:*** Go over communication guidelines with the couple, then ask one partner to speak by sharing a brief story while the other person actively listens. Coach the listener to improve different areas of listening skills as you observe them. Then, have them switch roles.

- ***Intervention:*** When you notice the couple not utilizing the communication guidelines, quickly intervene, remind them of what to do instead, then return them to the conversation.

HARD Conversations

After a rupture in the relationship, use the HARD conversation model. Describe how you can try out each step in the model:

- **Halt:** Pause the conversation as soon as you notice it is going off track. Depending on how reactive the conversation is, ask for a restart or take a break.

- **Attend:** Attend to attachment needs. You can do this by letting your partner know you love them and can continue the conversation after the break.

- **Repair:** After the break, offer repair to your partner by apologizing, offering affection, using humor, taking responsibility, or asking for a restart.

- **Debrief:** Talk together about what went wrong in the initial conversation and agree on one thing you could each do differently next time.

Building a Secure Relationship

A secure relationship is marked by a deep emotional connection and trust. In secure relationships, partners consistently exhibit safety and trust, open communication, empathy, emotional accessibility, effective communication, co-regulation, shared goals and values, constructive conflict resolution, physical affection, consistency, reliability, playfulness, and attachment security, where both partners feel assured of each other's support.

Consistency, not perfection, is key in creating a stable emotional foundation. Whether partners have insecure or secure attachment styles, they can develop security by adopting secure relationship behaviors, including emotional attunement, responsiveness, and unwavering commitment.

Focusing on these areas enhances the overall safety and fulfillment of the relationship.

Session Guidance

- ***Assessment:*** Explore the clients' attachment histories and observe attachment-related behaviors, noting signs of trust and responsiveness.
- ***Psychoeducation:*** Educate the couple on attachment theory and secure relationship components.
- ***Intervention:*** Identify the relationship's strengths and weaknesses. Select one area of weakness to work on for at least a week and offer guidance for improvement.

Building a Secure Relationship*

Secure relationships involve the following:

- ❑ Safety and trust
- ❑ Open communication
- ❑ Empathy
- ❑ Emotional accessibility
- ❑ Emotional support
- ❑ Effective communication
- ❑ Co-regulation
- ❑ Shared goals and values
- ❑ Constructive conflict resolution
- ❑ Physical affection
- ❑ Consistency and reliability
- ❑ Playfulness and fun
- ❑ Attachment security ("I know you are there for me")

1. **Check off your relationship's strengths.**
2. **Circle the areas you would like to improve.**
3. **Put a star next to the area you most want to improve, and focus for one week on improving this area.**

*Adapted from: Tatkin, S. (2012). *Wired for love: How understanding your partner's brain and attachment style can help you defuse conflict and build a secure relationship.* New Harbinger.

Windows and Walls

In relationships, there are **windows**, representing open communication and emotional intimacy, and **walls**, symbolizing emotional boundaries protecting the relationship.

Reverse windows occur when one partner confides in someone outside the relationship, potentially indicating emotional infidelity. An example might be a spouse discussing a conflict in their marriage with a coworker but not with their partner.

Reverse walls represent emotional distance or secrecy within a relationship. An example might be a partner who stops sharing information and excludes their partner from their life, like not inviting them to work events.

Couples should monitor their use of windows and walls to guard against potential infidelity.

Session Guidance

- ***Assessment:*** Note any walls from secrecy or emotional distance and assess whether the couple shows more openness to others (reverse windows).
- ***Psychoeducation:*** Explain how reverse windows or reverse walls can lead to betrayal and harm the relationship.
- ***Identification:*** Point out any reverse windows or reverse walls, encouraging an open dialogue.

Windows and Walls

Exploring Emotional Closeness and Boundaries in a Relationship*

WINDOWS

Windows are anything that helps you be seen openly by your partner:

- Open communication
- Time and space for the relationship
- Vulnerability
- Honesty

WALLS

Walls act as boundaries around the relationship to keep the relationship safe:

- Sharing appropriate information with others
- Protecting time, energy, and space for the relationship

REVERSE WINDOWS

Reverse windows are anything that opens a couple to betrayal:

- Sharing more information with others than with your partner
- Confiding in someone other than your partner
- Breaches of emotional intimacy in the primary relationship

REVERSE WALLS

Reverse walls are when the wall moves between the partners:

- Emotional distance
- Hiding information
- Defensiveness
- Evasiveness
- Keeping your partner "out"

* Adapted from: Glass, S. P., & Staeheli, J. C. (2003). *Not "just friends": Protect your relationship from infidelity and heal the trauma of betrayal.* Free Press.

Boundaries versus Control

Boundaries are healthy guidelines set to protect individual autonomy and maintain respect within a relationship. They empower both partners by promoting open communication and mutual consent.

Control, on the other hand, seeks to dominate and manipulate, often at the expense of a partner's autonomy. It stifles open communication and can lead to an unhealthy power dynamic.

Boundaries help couples know what they can expect so that they can rely on each other and feel secure in the relationship. When couples don't have healthy boundaries, there is a higher likelihood for resentment, distance, and infidelity.

Note: Helping couples understand this concept can be especially helpful during premarital counseling. It is imperative after a betrayal.

Session Guidance

- ***Assessment:*** Notice if the couple is violating any boundaries or calling something a boundary that is actually control.
- ***Feedback:*** Let the couple know that you are noticing some issues with boundaries.
- ***Psychoeducation:*** Talk to the couple about the difference between boundaries and control (if there is an issue with control).
- ***Exploration:*** Ask questions to better understand how they tend to implement boundaries and what they understand about boundaries.
- ***Exercise:*** Using each of the boundary types, have the couple rate from 1 to 5 how well they are doing with boundaries, with 1 being not having boundaries at all and 5 being strong boundaries.
- ***Homework:*** Have the couple choose one boundary type to work on.

Boundaries versus Control

	Boundaries	Control
Personal Space	• Respecting needs for alone time • Respecting areas of the home that are your partner's (e.g., their office)	• Demanding constant attention • Not allowing your partner to have their own personal space
Privacy	• Allowing your partner to have private thoughts and spaces • Not going through their personal devices or snooping	• Demanding passwords and constant access • Demanding your partner share all their private thoughts • Monitoring their phone*
Emotional Boundaries	• Respecting your partner's emotional experience • Keeping personal vulnerabilities sacred	• Putting words into your partner's mouth about their emotional experience • Using vulnerabilities against them • Using emotions to manipulate (e.g., guilt tripping)
Communication	• Setting limits on the type of language used during conversation • Having limits around how long a topic can be avoided	• Using silent treatment to get your way • Using hurtful language to get your way
Time Management	• Respecting your partner's time • Balancing individual versus couple time	• Telling your partner how they can spend their time • Not allowing individual time for hobbies and interests
Relational	• Having space to create healthy relationships outside of the relationship • Using windows and walls effectively • Only sharing appropriate information about your partner to others	• Isolating and controlling your partner so they cannot have outside relationships • Reversing walls • Oversharing information about your partner and your relationship**

* After a betrayal, a therapist might recommend temporary changes regarding privacy boundaries.
** If there is abuse, a therapist might recommend changes in what you share with others so you can get support.

Triangulation

Triangulation is when, instead of addressing conflicts directly, one or both partners draw a third person or issue into a relationship to alleviate tension and anxiety.

Examples of triangulation include seeking advice from friends during disagreements, using a child as a messenger instead of talking to your partner, or badmouthing a partner to a parent.

While it can be necessary at times, triangulation should be done with boundaries and the goal of resolving the issue directly. Trustworthy advisers should be chosen, and negative discussions about the relationship should be limited.

Triangulation harms relationships by hindering issue resolution, potentially betraying the partner's trust, and being unfair to the third party. Healthy relationships prioritize open and honest communication between partners as the first step in problem-solving.

Session Guidance

- ***Assessment:*** During therapy with a couple, assess if you notice patterns of triangulation. Identify the different triangles you or they have observed entering their relationship.
- ***Psychoeducation:*** If you notice triangulation in the relationship, ask the couple to pause, point out that they are using triangulation, and describe what it is.
- ***Exploration:*** Ask each partner how they feel about the triangulation in the relationship.
- ***Coaching:*** Be curious about why they don't communicate directly and then coach them to deal with tense topics with each other, rather than with outsiders.

Triangulation

Understanding Triangulation in Relationships

Map out a triangle that has entered into your relationship.

Partner A: ______________________

Partner B: ______________________

Third Party: ______________________

Emotional Bank Account

Every relationship includes an "emotional bank account." Think of it as an imaginary ledger tracking emotional deposits and withdrawals. Maintaining a healthy balance can counteract the impact of hurtful experiences, which tend to linger more powerfully than positive ones. To keep your emotional bank account positive, make consistent deposits and quickly repair withdrawals. Small, daily actions matter most.

Deposits

- Acts of kindness, appreciation, compliments
- Respect, especially during disagreements
- Quality time, responsiveness, collaboration
- Constructive conflict resolution, reliability

Withdrawals

- Hurtful words, avoidance, neglect
- Disregarding a partner's needs and dreams
- Destructive communication, triangulation, negativity to others
- Broken promises, deceit

Session Guidance

- ***Intervention:*** Use the checklist to have a conversation with the couple about what they get enough of and what they want more of. Coach each partner to invite this feedback and hear it with openness and curiosity.

Emotional Bank Account

The following are actions that fill the emotional bank account and make your relationship rich. Check what you have enough of, circle what you want more of, and talk about it with your partner.

- ❑ Affectionate notes or texts
- ❑ Ample time together
- ❑ Apologies
- ❑ Being on each other's side
- ❑ Being romantic
- ❑ Celebrating important moments
- ❑ Collaboration
- ❑ Consideration of each other's opinions
- ❑ Complimenting effort
- ❑ Complimenting intellect
- ❑ Complimenting appearance
- ❑ Complimenting character
- ❑ Cuddling
- ❑ Curiosity
- ❑ Dates
- ❑ Easing your partner's load
- ❑ Encouraging words
- ❑ Expressing trust
- ❑ Forgiveness
- ❑ Fun
- ❑ Gifts
- ❑ Good boundaries
- ❑ Helping each other
- ❑ Holding hands
- ❑ Hugs
- ❑ Initiating connection
- ❑ Kisses
- ❑ Knowing your spouse's "favorites"
- ❑ Massages
- ❑ Laughing together
- ❑ Novel experiences
- ❑ Play
- ❑ Offering encouragement
- ❑ Paying attention
- ❑ Participating in common activities
- ❑ Phone-free time
- ❑ Planning excursions
- ❑ Reassurance
- ❑ Remembering important dates
- ❑ Respect
- ❑ Responsibility taking
- ❑ Saying "I love you"
- ❑ Saying "thank you"
- ❑ Shared goals
- ❑ Showing interest in stories
- ❑ Showing interest in each other's passions
- ❑ Solving problems together
- ❑ Supporting each other's individual goals
- ❑ Surprises
- ❑ Thoughtful gestures
- ❑ Vacations
- ❑ Validation
- ❑ Vocal admiration

Fostering Intimacy

Intimacy is the feeling of closeness between people. There are six types of intimacy:

- **Sexual:** Physical pleasure and desire
- **Physical:** Nonsexual touch and physical closeness (e.g., hugs, kisses, cuddling)
- **Emotional:** Sharing feelings and a sense of trust
- **Spiritual:** Connecting on beliefs and values
- **Intellectual:** Sharing thoughts and stimulating conversations
- **Experiential:** Novelty, creating memories, shared activities

No one person will fulfill all types of intimacy for an individual. For example, you might have deep intellectual closeness with a friend while experiencing strong physical intimacy with your partner. When a relationship feels lonely, it often means a crucial intimacy type is lacking. Identifying these areas and taking small steps can help enhance intimacy and reduce loneliness.

Not everyone desires the same types of intimacy in a relationship. For example, one partner might desire more experiential intimacy while the other might desire more emotional intimacy. Partners should work together to support each other's desired needs for closeness.

Session Guidance

- ***Psychoeducation:*** Provide information about the different intimacy types.
- ***Intervention:***
  - Have the couple rate each area individually and share.
  - Ask them to choose an intimacy area to focus on.
  - Plan a small step toward building that intimacy that would add +1 to the current rating.
  - Emphasize gradual, consistent progress.

Fostering Intimacy

There are at least six types of intimacy. Rate each area from 1 to 10 (with 1 representing very low satisfaction and 10 representing very high satisfaction) using the chart below. Then, choose one area to improve by 1 point. Once that area is improved, move to the next area.

There are many types of intimacy

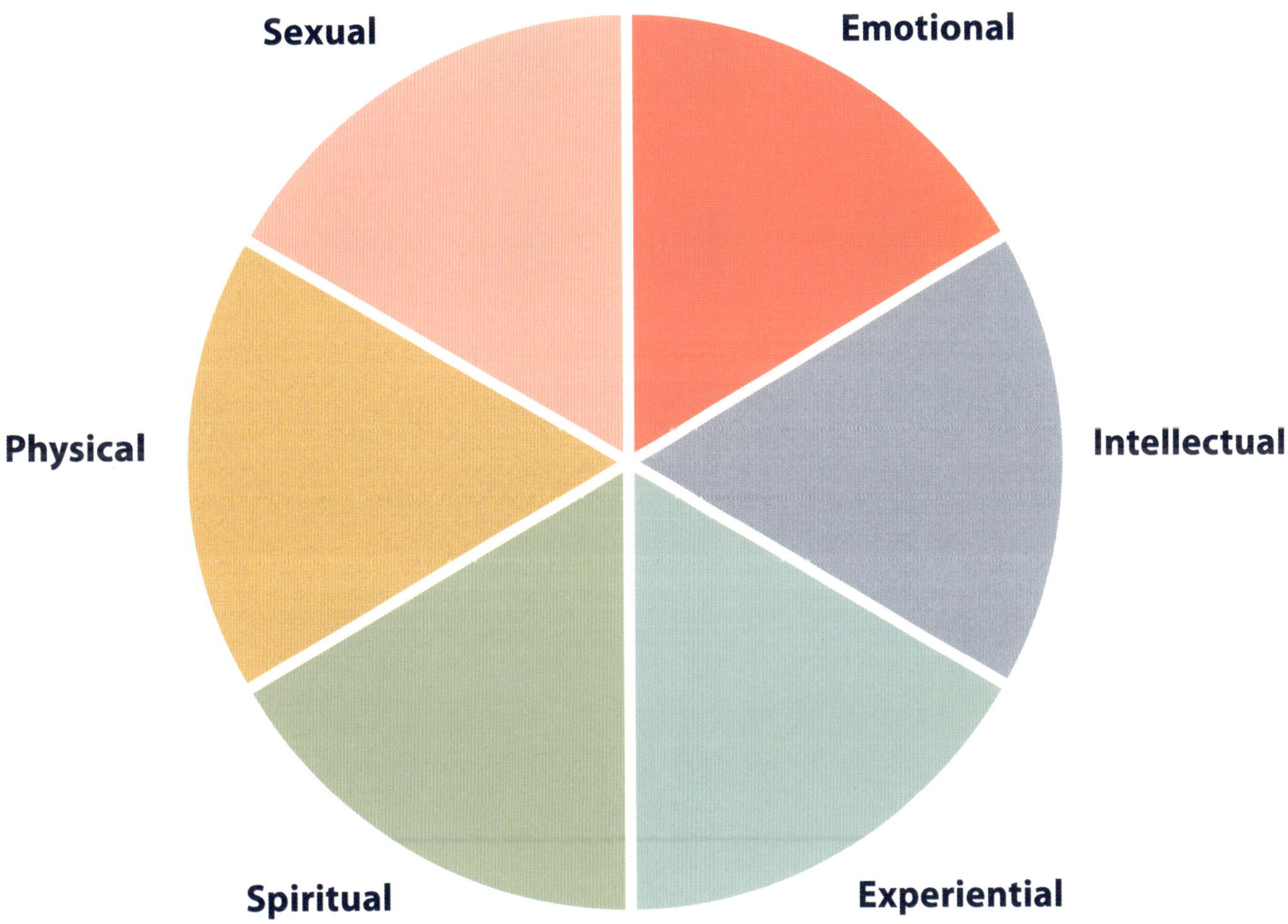

Mental Load Checklist

Mental load refers to the invisible and often overwhelming burden of managing numerous tasks, responsibilities, and decisions in daily life. It includes everything from organizing schedules and household chores to remembering important dates and emotional labor within relationships. Because there will always be things to remember, there will always be a mental load. It becomes a problem when one partner in a relationship carries a disproportionate share of this load, leading to stress, burnout, strained communication, and resentment.

To address the mental load, couples need to:

- Acknowledge the imbalance, avoiding defensiveness and criticism
- Work together to redistribute tasks in a way that feels fair (fair matters more than equal)
- Show appreciation for each other's efforts
- Commit to making change and have patience while it occurs

Session Guidance

- ***Assessment:*** Identify mental load disparities through observation or the checklist provided.
- ***Psychoeducation:*** Explain the concept of the mental load, provide task examples, and highlight its impact on relationships.
- ***Coaching:*** Help each partner develop empathy for how the mental load is impacting their partner.
- ***Intervention:*** Use the checklist to initiate a conversation about mental load equity. Address personal boundaries, facilitate task redistribution discussions by helping them negotiate, and guide the couple to avoid the Four Horsemen.

Mental Load Checklist

If you are responsible for researching, remembering, organizing, delegating, noticing, planning, or reminding others about a task, then you are carrying the mental load. Partner A, put a star next to the tasks you carry the mental load for more than 75% of the time. Partner B, put a check mark next to the tasks you carry the mental load for more than 75% of the time.

Financial Management

- ❑ Budgeting
- ❑ Paying bills
- ❑ Tracking expenses
- ❑ Managing investments
- ❑ Tax planning

Household Management

- ❑ Grocery shopping
- ❑ Cooking
- ❑ Cleaning
- ❑ Home maintenance
- ❑ Organizing
- ❑ Trash and recycling

Childcare and Parenting

- ❑ Scheduling
- ❑ School-related tasks
- ❑ Childcare
- ❑ Health
- ❑ Social activities

Healthcare

- ❑ Scheduling and attending medical appointments
- ❑ Managing medications
- ❑ Health insurance
- ❑ Health concerns

Relationships

- ❑ Birthdays
- ❑ Special occasions
- ❑ Maintaining relationships
- ❑ Together time
- ❑ Events
- ❑ Rituals

Time Management

- ❑ Schedules and routines
- ❑ Prioritizing tasks
- ❑ Reminders and alarms
- ❑ Calendar

Emotional Labor

- ❑ Providing emotional support to others
- ❑ Emotional well-being
- ❑ Stress
- ❑ Mediating conflicts

Technology and Info

- ❑ Passwords
- ❑ Tech issues
- ❑ News and events
- ❑ Digital files and data

Safety and Security

- ❑ Home security
- ❑ Identity theft prevention
- ❑ Emergency preparedness

Managing Major Life Changes

- ❑ Births
- ❑ Deaths
- ❑ Divorces

Travel

- ❑ Itineraries
- ❑ Booking
- ❑ Logistics

Joy

- ❑ Games
- ❑ Play
- ❑ Optimism
- ❑ Date nights
- ❑ Decorating
- ❑ Traditions

Other

- ❑ ____________________
  ____
- ❑ ____________________
  ____

Taking Breaks in Arguments

Sometimes, the advice "never go to bed angry" isn't the best approach. When arguments get heated, taking a break can prevent further damage to your relationship and make conversations more productive.

Couples need to agree on ground rules prior to a break. Otherwise, the break could be experienced as punishment, control, or abandonment.

Both partners need to work together to make a break effective:

- The person initiating the break needs to work to ensure their request isn't being used as punishment or to avoid a conversation. To build trust, they need to return to the conversation after they have calmed down.
- For the partner receiving the request, they should accept the request, even when it is hard, and take the break.

Session Guidance

- ***Assessment:*** Pay attention to when a couple needs to take a break.
- ***Psychoeducation:*** Let the couple know during a session that having a plan for taking breaks is healthy.
- ***Intervention:***
  - If you notice the couple needs to utilize breaks when they are flooded, help them come up with break ground rules in session, using the prompts provided.
  - They should work together to come up with ground rules for how to request a break, an acceptable break duration (between 20 minutes and 24 hours), self-soothing, and reconnecting after the break.

Taking Breaks in Arguments

When arguments get heated, taking a break can prevent further damage to your relationship and make conversations more productive.

Our Ground Rules	Self-Soothing Examples
• We will request a break by ______________________.	• Art (drawing, making music, etc.) • Breathing • Dancing
• We agree the break will last at least ________ (minutes/hours) and no more than ______________________.	• Gardening • Guided relaxation/meditation • Exercise • Journaling/writing
• During the break, we both agree to self-soothe and disengage from each other.	• Listening to music • Muscle relaxation • Walking the dog
• After the break, we will re-engage by ______________________.	• Watching TV • Sleeping

Avoid During the Break
• Coming back to the conversation too soon
• Continuing to engage (texting, calling, walking back into the room to talk)
• Doing potentially harmful activities during self-soothing time (drinking, gambling, etc.)
• Talking badly about your partner to other people
• Ruminating about the issue

Repair

Learning to repair is essential for maintaining healthy relationships. Repair can occur during or after an argument and plays a vital role in resolving conflicts.

During the argument, recognize signs of escalation, hurt feelings, misguided statements, compromised positions, disconnection, dysfunctional communication patterns like the Four Horsemen, or repetitive cycles. Offering repair in these moments can prevent further damage.

After an argument, initiate repair if you sense any harm caused, whether it's defensiveness, criticism, or an unsatisfactory conclusion. Apologize or reflect on the issues that arose.

Repair can take various forms, including offering apologies, using affection, introducing humor, requesting a redo, allowing negotiation, taking a break, assuming accountability, listening, or sharing feelings.

By consistently offering repair, you build safety, security, and trust within the relationship.

Session Guidance

- ***Psychoeducation:*** Explain the importance of in-the-moment and post-argument repair when you see the need.
- ***Exercises:***
    - Have the couple recall past situations requiring repair.
    - Ask each partner to identify the type of repair they prefer to make and the type they appreciate receiving.

Repair

Use repair during an argument when:	Use repair after an argument when:
• You notice escalation • You say something misguided • You notice your partner is hurting • You or your partner feel withdrawn or disconnected • You notice patterns, like going in circles • You catch yourself utilizing poor communication habits, like the Four Horsemen • You catch yourself avoiding compromise and negotiation/being stubborn	• Escalation occurred during the argument • Feelings need to be addressed • Connection needs to be rebuilt • You left a conversation without common ground • There is lingering resentment • You reflect and recognize your contribution to the problem • The argument ended without resolution • You gain perspective • Your projections are more clear

Examples of Repair

Circle the types of repair you prefer to make and put a star by the types you appreciate receiving.

Apologizing: "I am sorry"	**Affection:** "I love you," "Can I give you a hug?"	**Trying again:** "That came out wrong; let me try again"
Break: "Let's take a break"	**Negotiation:** "Okay, I am willing to consider that," "Tell me more"	**Accountability:** "Yikes, that was wrong of me"
Humor: Lighthearted comments	**Listening:** "Please tell me—I want to listen"	**Sharing emotions:** "I feel really sad right now"

Curiosity

In daily life, curiosity is a vital skill. Over time, couples may show less curiosity, assuming they know each other's thoughts, feelings, daily experiences, and aspirations. They should remember that their own efforts to engage can "make" their partner stay perpetually interesting.

During challenging conversations, it can be hard to remain curious, as people often become fixated on defending their own viewpoints rather than listening to their partner's perspective.

Couples must consciously strive to stay curious. Curiosity fosters connection, defuses conflict, promotes understanding, reduces assumptions, and facilitates continuous growth and connection in the relationship.

Many couples struggle with curiosity because they are uncertain how to ask genuinely inquisitive questions. It's essential to recognize that not all questions are equally effective.

Session Guidance

- ***Psychoeducation*:** Highlight the significance of curiosity and explain the value of open questions in fostering it.
- ***Practice*:**
  - ***Non-conflict Scenario:*** Have one partner inquire about the other's day to discover something new.
  - ***Conflict Scenario:*** Demonstrate curiosity by modeling open-ended questions and guide the couple to use such questions during their conversation to enhance empathy and understanding.

Curiosity

People are interesting when you are interested!

Curiosity is essential for couples in daily life. During moments of peace, couples can utilize curiosity to maintain a sense of closeness. During conflict, curiosity helps build empathy, understanding, common ground, and solutions.

To be curious, utilize open-ended questions rather than closed-ended questions or "gotcha" questions.

Open-Ended Questions ✅	Closed-Ended Questions ❌	Gotcha Questions ❌
Begin with words or phrases like "what," "how," "where," or "tell me about"	Begin with words like "is," "are," "did," or "will"	Begin with phrases like "isn't it true that" or "but didn't you say that"
Request more information about thoughts, feelings, experiences, or opinions	Are yes/no questions	Are adversarial in nature and are utilized to point out mistakes, flaws, or misstatements
Encourage conversations	Encourage sharing of specific facts	Intended to trap someone in an inconsistency in order to "win" an argument
Example: *What are your thoughts about our relationship lately?*	Example: *Did you go to work yesterday?*	Example: *You say you want to go to your mom's for the holiday, but didn't you tell me last week you hate being around your family?*

Negotiation

When couples disagree, one of the biggest pitfalls is trying to "win" the argument. Instead, couples should try to work together to merge their preferences and beliefs to create "win/win" outcomes.

To have a win/win outcome, couples need to learn the art of negotiation, which includes:

- **Relationship building:** Communicating in a fair, approachable, empathetic, and, at times, light and playful manner.
- **Exploration:** Having a structured conversation that includes each person's perspective, wants, needs, and ideas and creative options for problem-solving.
- **Temporary resolution:** The couple should try to always walk away with a temporary agreement. We say "temporary" because it is easier to agree to something that you are confident can change if it doesn't work.
- **Continued discussion:** The couple should come up with a time frame for checking back in with each other.

Session Guidance

- ***Intervention:***
    - When a couple is stuck on a disagreement, help them explore their perspectives, wants, needs, and ideas.
    - Then, have them come up with a creative resolution that merges their desired outcomes.
    - Last, ask them to set a date for checking in with each other about whether or not the resolution is working.

Negotiation

The issue we are trying to solve is: ______________________________

Exploration	**Resolution Ideas**
Include each of your needs in resolving this issue and your desired outcomes.	Include all ideas that would help you both to meet your needs.

Hints:

- If you get stuck coming up with a solution, ask the question "Where do we agree?" and start with the areas of agreement.
- Try to create a solution that includes all of your needs, recognizing you will likely have to give up some wants.

Resolution

We will check in with each other on this date to explore how well this resolution has been working: ______________________________